Alma Cleo Childress – 1927
Engagement Portrait

Hold Fast This Beauty

Hold Fast
This Beauty

By

Alma Childress Brown

Edited by Elizabeth Brown Mynatt

Earthtide
Publications

Library of Congress Catalog Number: 90-083485
ISBN No. 0-9622568-4-6

Printed in the United States of America

EARTHTIDE PUBLICATIONS,
Knoxville, Tennessee

To my children,

Robert and Liz

and in memory of

Alva Ross

1938

1926

ACKNOWLEDGEMENTS

The Blue and White

Christian Board of Publication

Clayton Daily News

Firestone News

Georgia State Poetry Society

The Knoxville Journal

The Knoxville News Sentinel

Let's Share

Little Ones

Milligan Stampede

Standard Publishing Company

Summer Treasure And Other Poems

The Pen Woman

World of Poetry

FOREWORD

"Go, Little Booke!..."

- G. Chaucer

Grandparents, Phoebe and George Hayes, C. 1918

CONTENTS

HOLD FAST THIS BEAUTY

PORTS AND HAPPY HAVENS

AH, LIFE WAS SWEET

LANES OF MEMORY

PHOTOGRAPHS

Brother Buford (L.) and Alma Cleo Childress – 1910

HOLD FAST THIS BEAUTY

"The White House," 1929 where Alma and Alva began married life.

RITUAL

Come in and close the door against the chill:
Although the fields are bathed in mellow light,
The days grow short, and here beneath the hill,
Deep shadows tell us of approaching night.
Then bring the wood, and on the clean-swept hearth,
Together let us kneel and lay the fire;
A homely ritual ancient as the earth,
And quieting some vague, unnamed desire.
Now spread the cloth and set the things for tea:
The fragile, flower-sprigged cups, the polished spoons;
Our hearts may garner deep serenity
Against all bleak and lonely afternoons.
For, oh, too soon the bloom of summer goes!
So let this fire become our winter rose.

NO WORDS

It is always different, always new,
This miracle of returning spring;
Never before such jeweled dew,
Such blue on a small bird's wing;

Never such heady fragrance under a moon,
Never such joyous coming of the birds,
And for the ruddy dawn and golden noon,
There are no adequate words.

There are no words at all to tell
Of the eager growth of stem and leaf,
Of tender buds that part and swell,
And the putting away of the heart's old grief.

IN DEFENSE OF THE SONNET

O lightsome sonnet, darling of the Muse,
Most graceful form conceived in Helicon,
By Spenser loved, by Milton put to use
To mourn his gift of sight so early gone;
Recording for all time Keats' wild surmise
On meeting Homer in fair realms of gold;
Employed by Shakespeare to immortalize
A love that would outlast a world grown old!

But poets of today will not be bound
By rigid forms constraining poesy,
And find the "sonnet's scanty plot of ground"
Inhibits those who sing of liberty.
O ancient song, I find, with sad surprise
How faithless Fortune is, how blind men's eyes!

SPRING: TWO SONNETS

I

Not gently as the autumn came about
But with a burst of bud and song came spring,
Announced by clear and sprightly trumpeting
Of golden-throated daffodils and shout
Of children in the street. Now put to rout
Is brooding winter thought. Tired hearts take wing
And up the steepy air with thrushes sing,
While crocuses and pansies dare peek out.
I know, I know you say the theme is old,
That poets have exhausted every word
To paint this miracle in varied hue;
That charms of spring have been too often told,
And one is wearied of "Sweet flower and bird,"
Yet who can ably sing the earth made new?

II

And could it be that all the winter through
The spirit was sustained by thought of these?
Clouds feather-soft against a brighter blue.
Pale chartreuse leaves unfolding on staid trees,
And hyacinths set in an ordered row
Like rosy candles lighted to new faith
That lifts its wings above the melting snow,
More tenuous than fragile, misty wraith;
The canopy of dusk let softly down,
And one gold star pinned to the velvet west;
Above the tall red chimneys of the town
The dark swifts spiraling downward to their rest,
And sparrows in the vine leaves at the door;
All these the heart knew hunger for once more.

4

IN PRAISE OF BLUE

Now is the time of azure skies,
Of violets eagerly opening eyes,
Of shiny boats, sails fresh and new,
Skimming lake waters of sparkling blue.
Indigo bunting, bluebird and jay,
On swift blue wings all take their way.

And from the garden's orderly beds,
Blue hyacinths proudly lift their heads.
Did the Master like this color, too?
And was His mother's dress bright blue?
Oh, I like to think when just a lad
That often in blue He went cleanly clad.

THE CONSTANTS

The sun comes up with an orange glow
Dispelling grey mists of dawn.
In a stealthy nighttime maneuver,
Dandelions conquer the lawn.
The brook and river keep their tryst,
As they journey out to sea.
The farmer begins spring plowing,
While the crow claims his own tall tree.
Children discard their winter wraps,
Violets bank bare hills with blue,
Flocks of robins come up from the South,
And I come down with flu.

INTIMATIONS

Warm and golden in the sun,
Bright green the tender grass,
And gentle are the little winds
That whisper as they pass.

And, oh, how blithe the robin's song,
The peeper's note, how clear;
How sweet, how sure, the many signs
That tell us spring is here.

But if I could not feel the sun,
Nor see the blue bird's wing,
I think I'd know, because my heart
Would surely bid me sing.

BACKYARD DRAMA

Dogwoods come to bloom at every turn.
In lively chorus small birds blithely sing,
And you, lithe acrobat, now bring your act
To the radiant, colored pageantry of spring.
With wondrous speed you scale the tallest oak
To nibble a tender bud; you turn, you twist
And flick your handsome plume in fine disdain,
Knowing elation of the veteran aerialist.
Now comes the measured leap to grasp a twig--
I freeze, entranced, and watch with quickened breath:
With unmatched grace you swiftly right yourself,
While far below, it could have been--sudden death!

I HAD FORGOTTEN

The autumn was so gloriously attired
    In orange, scarlet, gold and russet brown,
I said I cannot bear to see
    The last bright leaf come down.

And why, I questioned grieving,
    Must all this beauty go?
For I had forgotten the loveliness
    Of softly drifted snow.

I had forgotten the smell of blue wood smoke
    Above the friendliness of open fires;
The way of tall, dark pines
    Like thin cathedral spires,
Bravely calm and lifted high
    Against a turquoise evening sky.

HAIKU

I

The late August storm
Brought this empty bird's nest down;
Summer ends too soon.

II

Two birds wheel as one,
Southward, down a darkling sky,
Fleeing winter's wrath.

PASSAGES

No longer can King Winter hold in thrall
His loyal troops that bow at his command
To hurl their icy spears in mighty band,
And buffet trees and ships with angry squall.
Now April with her ruffled parasol
Trips through wet grass and from a dainty hand
Strews daffodils across a greening land,
And with her radiant smile she blesses all.
Then, like a choir of distant violins,
The happy thrushes' welcome trill begins.
Blue sky and sun and fragrant hyacinth bloom,
With magic touch disperse all lingering gloom.
Pink buds on peach and apple trees appear,
Yet doves chant one sad song at Winter's bier.

POETRY OF EARTH

For those who will but pause to hear and see
The poetry of earth is everywhere,
In murmured chant of languid, sun-warmed bee,
In elms that lift green banners to the air.
At every turn earth's beauty begs to speak
The quiet strength of gently rolling hills,
Vague mystery of distant mountain peak,
Prim grace of pansy, gold of daffodil.

The poetry of earth is free to share,
Its message written clearly for the one
Who seeks it in the jeweled, rain-fresh air,
In tenuous river mist or ancient stone;
Who finds the ecstasy in song of birds
And couples it to silver-winged words.

THE SMALL AFFAIRS OF EARTH

The small affairs of earth make up my day:
Watering plants upon a window sill;
Pausing to admire the fountain spray
Of leafy elm trees on a distant hill;
Arranging pansies in an old blue bowl
That graced Grandmother's sideboard long ago,
A prized reminder of a gentle soul
Whose love of common things I think I know.

And as the good day passes, friends drop by
For tea and conversation. Thrushes sing
Their vesper hymn, and from the evening sky
The radiant colors fade. Remembering
Each golden hour with gratitude, I say:
The small affairs of earth make up my day.

DOWN SOUTH

Creamy bloom on the dark magnolia bough,
  Fields of cotton, music of rustling corn,
Crape-myrtle petals falling on the grass,
  The song of mockingbirds at early morn.

A wild rose hedge by a pasture fence
  And shade, leaf-sweet and cool,
Where willows bend above patient cows
  Knee deep in a blue-green pool.

The smell of mint, and vanilla grass
  From a field of new-mown hay,
All these in shimmering sunlight
  Make a Southern summer day.

SUMMER FIELDS

I left the four walls of my house
      To walk the fields today,
And I marked the Queen Anne's Lace
      That grew beside the way.
With careful, practiced fingers
      I pushed the bloom apart,
To find a wreath of flowerets -
      The brilliant ruby heart.

Daisies and buttercups I saw,
      And flowers I could not name,
While orange milkweed on the hill
      Was brighter than a flame.
The wind was sweet with clover and mint;
      White clouds sailed down the sky;
The sun lay warm on the furrowed land,
      And I heard a skylark cry.

I left the four walls of my house
      To walk the fields today,
And the memory of all the things I saw,
      For weeks and weeks will stay.

HAIKU

Scarlet cardinal,
Nestled on a snowy branch,
Winter day's delight.

HOLD FAST THIS BEAUTY

All suddenly the lovely summer ends,
     And like a queen grown weary of her reign,
Now swiftly from her golden throne descends,
     Nor cares to mount its jeweled steps again.
A late rose blooms beside the worn brick walk;
     The air at noon is clear as crystal glass;
A drowsy bee falls from an aster stalk,
     And crickets murmur softly in the grass.

O heart, hold fast this beauty you have known,
     For summer wealth is made of transient things;
Today, a scented blossom bright, full-blown,
     Tomorrow, flown as birds on silent wings,
And soon this wooded, fern-sweet path you know
     Will sleep beneath a weight of drifted snow.

NOW EXTINCT

It could have been just such a day as this:
Dogwoods stitching barren hills with lace,
And redbud torches lighting fern-banked trails;
When you, the last of all your airy race,
Wheeled forth against a silent sky
At misty dawn, leaving your twiggy nest,
To feel the upward thrust of buoyant air
Against your softly iridescent breast.

Oh, beautiful your flight above the fields!
Yet no one there to cry you swift alarm
Before the skulking enemy advanced
To raise a jubilant, practiced arm,
And bring you spinning down, the proud, the free,
To lie at last a piteous broken thing;
Your fate forever sealed by that bright drop
Of waxen red that stains a crumpled wing.

AUTUMN'S WAY

I must go out of my house
This early autumn day,
So bright, so tantalizing
In some compelling way.
The mellow sunlight warmly gleams
Through trembling, still-green trees.
Tall pines are quivering silver
In the gently playful breeze,
Pink petals from crape myrtle blooms
Embroider fading grass,
And from his nest the cricket's chant
Grows silent as I pass.

The color of a lively jay
That flashes swiftly by,
Rivals the rich vibrant blue
Of a faraway cloudless sky.
From his lofty, hidden perch now comes
The insistent call of a crow.
Why is this dark one a harbinger
Of winter woods, of snow?
Must I go in now to perform
Some demanding, petty chore,
And leave such autumn treasure
Outside my shuttered door?

DAY IN AUTUMN

The sky is clear
    The sun is bright,
The wild birds fly
    Through dazzling light.

By lane and path
    On every hand,
In scarlet dress
    The maples stand.

The hickory sways
    A thing of grace,
A radiant queen
    In golden lace.

The cricket hides
    In sun-lit grass
And murmurs his song
    For all who pass.

A rare mild day,
    All blue and gold--
How distant seems
    The winter cold!

SOFTLY NOW THE AUTUMN RAIN

Softly now the autumn rain
    Falls through fading leaves.
For summer's sudden passing
    The lonely garden grieves.

On withered stalk of poppy
    And aster falls the rain;
Only the broken stem can tell
    Of summer's lovely train.

Upon the walk the maple leaves
    Lie wet and pumpkin bright;
A flash of blue in orchard trees
    Marks the jay's bold flight.

Against the misty, troubled sky,
    Fly the dusky crows;
The cornfield tents to which they wing
    Will soon be roofed by snows.

Oh, Autumn, soon the gentle snow
    In sleep will fold your leaves
And thus will peace as softly come
    To heal the heart that grieves.

PREDICTION

The pale sun bathes familiar hills,
    The river flows with soundless sweep,
Across tall pines the blue smoke drifts,
    And fields are lost in sleep.

Thin sunlight can not warm an earth
    So clothed in ragged brown;
Above the corn land hungry crows
    Are flying up and down.

A few tenacious, withered leaves
    To boughs of white oaks cling,
The maple bends to stinging wind,
    And winter still is king.

Only silent winter birds -
    Cardinal, sparrow and jay - are here,
But something within awakes and sings,
    And tells me Spring is near,

With snow-white petals drifting,
    And brooks in meadows singing,
With miracles on every hand,
    And hope in tired hearts springing.

SILENT MORNING

The early morning light came with a glow,
Ethereal and luminously bright,
Proclaiming that a miracle by night
Had blanketed the earth with pristine snow.
How changed were all familiar things! Each row
Of cottages now roofed with layered white;
All ugly scars completely healed, no blight
To mar the skies above nor earth below.
From neighboring chimneys, wispy blue smoke curled
Adds deeper silence to a silent world.
Late autumn's broken stalk and leafless tree
Are now a-bloom in wondrous purity.
New snow can rival softest ermine gown,
Yet snap a lofty pine and bring it down.

THEME WITH VARIATIONS

On a mellow autumn afternoon,
I hear the cricket softly croon
From a tuft of drying grass,
As I leisurely pass.

But in the hour of winter night,
With all my world grown hushed and white,
Suddenly from some chink in the wall,
The cricket's strident song
Comes on too strong!

Alma, Alva and Betty (Liz) – 1940

PORTS AND HAPPY HAVENS

Home Place, C. 1914
Grandmother Ellen Childress on front porch

HOME PLACE

 he ancient house sits there below the hill;
Outside its door remain worn steps of stone;
But happy voices that it knew are still.

Wild roses climb about the window sill;
Though wayward grasses claim the once-trim lawn,
The ancient house sits there below the hill.

Into its empty rooms old lilacs spill
Their dew-drenched sweet perfume at misty dawn,
But happy voices that it knew are still.

Late summer days now suddenly grow chill,
And robins leave come autumn's somber tone;
The ancient house sits there below the hill.

Then spring returns and here a daffodil
Beside the crooked garden path moss-grown,
But happy voices that it knew are still.

Ah! Fading grace remains and always will--
A queen whose ruined beauty lingers on;
The ancient house sits there below the hill,
But happy voices that it knew are still.

AT TINTAGEL

The young driver packed us into his Jeep,
And jolted down that rocky gulch
To the rim of the awesome chasm
Where, for centuries the turbulent waves
Have battered the Cornwall Coast.
High, high above the fury of the sea,
Crowning the forbidding cliff, we gasped in wonder
At the crumbling grey ruins of the Castle,
"The legendary birthplace of King Arthur."
Legendary? Ah, no! The place attests to greatness...

I like to think it's so. Here then was Arthur born,
The King who reigned in storied Camelot
With Guinevere (oh what sad fate!) his Queen, who
         loved him not.
The jostling ride to level ground again,
Our feet once more on grass soft and green,
Still shaken by the steep ascent,
And the wild beauty of the scene,
I had need of the simple reality:
Ripe red strawberries with clotted cream
And a cup of steaming tea.

POOR OPHELIA

While resting in the shade of the weeping willow
That hugged the blue lake's shore,
In my mind's eye I saw, I swear,
A comely maiden floating there,
Borne up by the willow's green-gold tresses
Commingled with her long golden hair.
Ah, evil days! Oh, what sad fate!
After the ecstasy, the vows of sweetest affection,
From this lord of high estate,
How could she comprehend the change, the dalliance
Of the charming prince?
Confused, plucking white daisy petals--
"He loves me, he loves me not."
Then came that monstrous cruel charge:
"Get thee to a nunnery!"
"The sweet bells jangled, out of tune," Oh, bleak
rejection.

For her, no high-flown "To be or not to be,"
But fleeing the stern gray walls of Elsinore,
And running barefoot in the early dew,
Down to the riffling water's edge,
She did what she had to do!
And so, dear sister, these long centuries dead,
I weave a garland of pansies and rue
For your pretty head.

DOROTHY WORDSWORTH'S
JOURNALS REVISITED

The roar of traffic from the avenue
Comes indistinctly through the summer night;
While midge-like cares of day are put to flight,
The city glows against the sky. _With you_
I walk beside still lakes of lapis blue,
Or see you in Dove Cottage, swept and bright,
Set out the things for tea by candlelight,
In preparation for the cherished few
You love and favor with your caring look.
And now our paths through Scottish glens unfold
By misty loch, and crag, and fern-sweet brook.
Oh, strange it is within my hands to hold
All that we have of you, a slender book,
"Poor earthly casket" of a mind's pure gold!

HAIKU

Sunset burns red-gold.
Street lamps blossom in the dusk,
Guiding footsteps home.

PORTRAIT OF JENNY LIND IN EVENING LIGHT

The April sky is tender blue; the shower
That came on suddenly is quickly spent.
Dark clouds that lingered in the west are rent
By late sun rays that at this witching hour,
Impartially caress green blade and bower,
And entering this quiet room where scent
Of lilac drifts, illumine the intent,
Bright gaze of her whose face is like a flower
Against the ruby velvet of her chair.
The strong yet gentle hands serenely lie,
And smooth as brown bird's shining wing the hair.
The slightly parted lips emit no sigh--
No golden notes imbue the listening air.
But, oh! such fame as hers can never die!

VILLANELLE: THE PINES OF ROME

How ageless stand the pines of Rome!
Protecting court and bustling street,
The past entwined in each green dome,

Fair shade to arch and marble tomb,
Cool tents for birds in summer heat.
How ageless stand the pines of Rome!

They bless the weary, miles from home,
Endure rough wind and chilling sleet,
The past entwined in each green dome.

Deep hidden roots pierce needled loam;
Bright poppies tremble at their feet.
How ageless stand the pines of Rome!

Staunch guard to ancient catacomb,
Beholding armies in retreat,
The past entwined in each green dome.

They sigh near fountains tumbling foam,
Delight young lovers where they meet.
How ageless stand the pines of Rome!
The past entwined in each green dome.

PRAYER FOR OUR COUNTRY

Eternal God, ruler of the universe,
So many strident voices are heard:
May we be still and quietly attuned
To your unerring, luminous word.

May the polar star of wisdom
And justice be our guide
To steer us clear of prejudice,
Arrogance and vain pride.

Let each individual strive to restore
The confidence of our nation,
That its stance in a world of differing views
Be worthy of emulation.

Help us guard our precious freedoms
And patiently learn to resolve
Grievous, perplexing problems
With understanding and love.

Let our homes be filled with bright laughter,
And should there come sorrows and tears,
Grant us courage, Lord, and grace
For all our days and years.

CLOUDS

*(For Georgia O'Keeffe)**

Pancakes in the sky,
On our backs we watch them move
Faraway, nearby.

TENNESSEAN IN TEXAS

For hours we drove through a bluebonnet sea;
The Texas sun came down brassy and hot
Until, eager, in mid-afternoon we came
At last to that storied spot--
The Alamo; shaded by live oak trees,
Set apart from the din of the street,
And bordered by quiet rose gardens,
Where fact and legend now meet.

Listed in bronze beyond those rugged walls,
In the shadowy light, we are startled to see
The many names of men who fiercely fought
Far from their native hills of Tennessee.
The horror of the battle scene returns;
Throats tighten with unshed tears; the sound
Of voice and footstep ceases now;
In awe we stand on bloodstained, holy ground.

* by Alma Brown and J. Ross Mynatt

IMPRESS: 1957

Oh, the buoyant air of California!
The scent of eucalyptus everywhere.
Leaning from a Sausalito balcony,
The retired businessman from the East,
In a moment of detachment
Believes that he will live forever.
Cottages go up in flames of red geraniums;
Stone walls are bowers of crimson bougainvillaea.
Evening and the iced-wool blanket
Slowly unrolls across the Bay,
Silencing the Golden City
In folds of chilling grey.
Up and down the boulevard the stiffened fronds
Of palms weep lonely tears.
Weary tourists sip champagne
At "The Top of the Mark."
And, Oh, the buoyant California air!
The heady scent of eucalyptus everywhere.

WINDOWS

A window is such a lovely thing
When it frames a white bird on the wing,
Or tall young maples in early spring.

A window may face the sunset's glow,
Or firs with branches bending low
Beneath a burden of clean white snow.

A window may frame the tender dawn,
Small children playing upon a lawn,
Or a starred blue sky when day is gone.

I wish today that my life might be
Forever as calm and orderly
As windows that look upon field and tree.

HAIKU

Bare boughs are bobbins
Wound with snow-white thread to spin
Miles of dogwood lace.

MOUNTAINS

When I grow weary with the stress of life,
 And clamor of the senseless hurry tries
My very soul, and I am sick of strife,
 To distant mountain heights I life my eyes;
And in their quiet strength and majesty,
 That change not from sun to burning sun,
A steadfast calm and timelessness I see
 That shames the fevered race men choose to run.

Then all my restless yearnings drop away,
 As notes fall from the bough where thrushes sing,
And peace as holy as the close of day
 Descends and folds me in her brooding wing.
Tall mountains rise above the fragrant sod
 And point me to the shining face of God.

STRICTLY RAPPING

(With Apologies to Edwin Newman)

Ed sez English now is inoperative,
That America has done her in;
Man, if that's how the cookie crumbles,
Spare the tears for a great has-been.

Like, I dig the American language;
It's the name of the game to rap.
Do your thing, play it smart, and keep your cool,
Or, plain, you're a weirdo---zap!

Don't bug me with erudite phrases;
If asked what it's all about,
In this time frame, y'know it's relevant
Just to let it all hang out.

To **** with structured restrictions;
No kidding, we're all OK.
At this point in time, old buddy,
Right on, and have a nice day!

TRIBUTE

Dick Cavett presents: "Isaac Bashevis Singer..."
Startled, I thought, a striking "ringer"
For Professor Alwin Thaler,
Friend, teacher, scholar,
Who led me to Shakespeare: the human condition
In comedy, history, tragedy AND the Kittredge Edition.
Alike in appearance, whimsical, kind;
Their lives one high adventure of the mind.

And how I loved this
When, according to rumor, Isaac Bashevis
Singer had said
He would not walk across the street
To meet
Sigmund Freud.
But when
pressed replied, half-smiling-frowning,
"Well, maybe across the street, but not to Flushing."

Issac Bashevis Singer was awarded the 1978 Nobel Prize for Literature.
Alwin Thaler (deceased) was a distinguished Professor of English
Literature at the University of Tennessee.

AFTERNOON OF A WEDDING

(Christ Church, St. Simons Island)

Through the Gothic arch of the stained glass window
The failing afternoon light
Softly rests on the kneeling pair,
The groom in summer blue, the bride in billowing white.
Their solemn vows are said, the music swells,
And from the door flung wide
Another handsome groom, another fairy-tale bride.
They hurry down the worn brick walk
Edged by roses, yellow, white and red,
Soundlessly strewing their velvet petals
On the sunken graves of the dead.
Above the celebrants, the giant oaks
In blessing extend their mammoth arms
That, come the springtime warmth, are laced
With new-green resurrection ferns.
Through the shadowy gloom of the tree tops,
A sudden flash of brilliant red
And chirking, raucous laughter reveal
The elusive presence of "Old Hammerhead."

Other prophets will pass this way
On famous Frederica Road
And bow their heads in benison,
Where long ago the Wesleys stood,
And in the shimmering warm April rain,
The resurrection ferns will come to life again.

TIME OUT

I've done my share of ceramics,
Of baskets and macrame;
Attended a gourmet cooking class,
And jogged a mile each day.

I've turned a sunny plot in spring,
Then planted onions and roses,
And tried my hand at painting,
In the style of Grandma Moses.

I've travelled to far Hawaii
And marvelled at plants and birds,
Then jetted above Grand Canyon -
Too awesome for poet's words.

I've knitted a cozy afghan,
And pieced a friendship quilt.
Now I'd like to sit and rock a spell
Without any feelings of guilt.

COMING BACK TO THE GOLDEN ISLES

Year after year, after year,
We gather our encumbrances and come back here
Where the golden grasses bend
And flow with the warm wind.
The palms and stunted pines
Steadfastly creep to hold their stand
Where the waves fall over against the glinting sand.

Our footsteps clatter down the wooden walk.
The old ones lead their dogs, while overhead,
The clamoring gulls circle and swoop to snatch
From the wary children's hands their scraps of bread.
A boat comes in, a boat goes slowly out and dissolves
Where sea and sky become one.
And for a moment, our pensive faces are bathed
In the last scarlet rays of the sun.
With blurring eyes in the cooling mist,
We watch the lumbering pelicans go by,
Skimming the blue-gray water
Under the gray-blue sky.
Even the youngest children know
What lies beyond "the boundless, deep blue sea";
Yet, as we seek the evening lights of the town,
We are haunted by some ancient, unsolved mystery.

One morning early, we gather our worthless
  shells and books unread,
Over the causeway, over the burnished marsh,
Our thoughts are our own. No words are said.
Then into the swaying Georgia pines, we meet the
Silver rain,
And we know that if our small world holds,
Next year, we will come to the Golden Isles again.

Mother,
Kate Blanche Hayes – 1903

Tintype of Father,
Robert Madison Childress – 1902

AH, LIFE WAS SWEET

Alma and Alva are married – 1929

THINGS UNSAID

e sit in a little world apart
Here in this dusk-filled room.
The firelight falls across the floor
And scatters the velvet gloom.
Your glance is on the roses by your chair;
I pour the fragrant tea,
And this hour will be remembered
For its sweet tranquility.
Our talk is of unimportant things,
And yet I understand
All things unsaid by the way you smile,
By the way you hold my hand.

THE DREAMER

The sifting dust collects
    Upon her polished floor;
Unheeded are the finger marks
    That show upon the door.

The spider spins his web
    Above the curving stair,
(His little silken net
    Looks so pretty there.)

The water in the kettle
    Has all boiled away;
The neighbors smile and look askance
    And then go on their way.

All her household ways
    Have gone from bad to worse,
While she sits dreaming by the fire
    Thumbing a book of verse.

HILLS

I know a hill, a leaning hill,
Where violets peep through
The velvet moss and tender grass,
Impearled with shining dew.

I know a hill, a tall green hill,
With pines upon its crest,
Where wind is music on the bough
And gray doves build their nest.

I know a hill, a sloping hill,
Where snow lies clean and new,
Where scars are hidden from the sight
And shadows are softly blue.

But, Oh, the cruel, stony hill,
Whereon one came to die,
In bitter pain, upon a tree
For such as you and I!

FIRST THANKSGIVING DAY

Blue wood smoke from those rustic homes
        Curled above tall pines to autumn skies;
While in warm kitchens happy laughter rang
        As strong hands baked brown loaves and pies.

But even as that brave and hardy band
        Gathered on their first Thanksgiving Day,
With family and loyal Indian friends
        About the feast, and lifted hearts to pray,

In thankfulness for bounteous gifts received,
        They knew that past the clearing, enemies,
Wild hungry beasts, and unknown savages
        Were lurking in the shadowy forest trees.

So has it been since history's early dawn;
        Each age presents its strange untried frontiers
In varied form to challenge and to lure
        The questing spirit of brave pioneers.

Today our enemies are not in forest glen,
        But in the minds and in the hearts of men.
Lead us, Oh God, before it grows too late,
        From ravages of war, from bonds of hate.

EVENING THOUGHT

To my left is the misty blue mountain;
    To my right is the highway where cars
Go in and out from the villages;
    Above me the evening's first stars.

Before me the deep greening valley
    Grows quiet as shadows descend,
And lamplight in white cottage windows
    Glows softly to mark the day's end.

Now sensing the peace of the moment
    And breathing its stillness I say:
I am glad of life and the chance it gives
    To love, to work, and to play.

A DAY IN WINTER

Oh, there is so much beauty to be seen
From dawn to lovely dawn,
I counted four bright cardinals today
Upon the snow-clad lawn.

Between high hills and down through shining fields,
Beneath a sudden burst of noonday sun,
A gleaming ribbon made of platinum,
I saw the river run.

And when the pale, gold sun had disappeared,
And all the white world suddenly grew still,
I saw outlined against the sunset sky,
A weathered farm house on a distant hill.

Then, as the purple dusk came softly down,
I saw a window glow with yellow light.
My heart gave thanks for all the day had brought,
And peace came stealing with the winter night.

PRESENTIMENT

Our love is like a candle flame:
Its steady glow
Is warm and bright, but candles have a way
Of burning low.
And so, if life should take unto itself again
This radiant thing it gave
To us for one brief shining hour,
I shall be brave.
And if I find that I must grope alone
Through some dark night,
I shall not flinch, but teach my heart to say,
"It was a lovely light."

Old Main – 1926
Emma Elizabeth Johnson at the grave of her husband,
Dr. Ashley Sidney Johnson

OLD MAIN

I am the Main Building
Of Johnson Bible College.
I am more than brick and mortar--
More than stone and wood and glass.
I am a child of faith and hope.
I am the answer to a strong man's prayer.
Up from the blackness of despair,
And the bitterness of frustration,
From the cold ashes of my predecessor
In triumph I arose.

I have seen many seasons come and go.
I have seen the hills tenderly green in spring--
Crowned with the snowy lace of blossoming dogwood.
I have dreamed through long golden summer afternoons.
I have seen the maples clothed in scarlet dress
When the spell of Indian summer held the land.
I know the feel of lashing winter gales,
The sting of flying snow against my face.

Warm sunlight, slanting through
My stained glass windows,
Has caressed the cheeks of fair young brides,
Has bathed the rapt faces
Of men and women at morning worship,
And rested, oh, so lightly, on the brows
Of loved ones in death.

Sometimes at midnight,
When the many shadows creep,
And it is very still--
But for the swish and murmur of the river--
A strong presence seems to linger near,
And I find myself listening for a once familiar step,
But then I remember, and I lean
A little more protectingly
Above the rugged granite marker
Glistening in the cold, white moonlight.

My corridors are deeply scarred
By the passing of many feet.
Throughout the years
I have remained steadfast in the purpose
For which I was created, and my doors
Are open day and night to poor young men--
As a mother hen covers her brood,
So have I sheltered these.
I have heard them laugh and weep,
I have seen them work and play.
I am the very center of the life
Of Johnson Bible College:
I am the Main Building.

HAIKU

Dove in the green wood,
Why on this glorious morn,
Do you sadly mourn?

PHOTOGRAPH

Here in this room, where morning sunbeams dance
  Into the shadow's cool, dim hiding place,
I pause to meet your earnest searching glance,
  Then stand and gaze upon your dear, dear face.
A white rose on your desk is in full bloom,
  Your books in place; these things you do not see,
But when I pace the full length of the room
  And back again, your blue eyes follow me.

Oh, wistful face, that does not care to turn
  To see the lace that slender maples make
Against the sky, nor stars that nightly burn
  But marks my every move, each step I take,
Would that I had the magic power to bring
  To breathing warmth this precious silent thing!

SLOW OF HEART

When Cleopas and that other one,
*   Whose name we do not know,*
Trod the dusty road to Emmaus
*   That day long years ago,*

Their hearts were sad as they communed,
*   And when the Stranger came to walk with them,*
They did not know that it was He who died
*   Upon a cross outside Jerusalem.*

Brave hopes were gone. Their eyes were blind,
*   And they were slow of heart to understand*
His promise to return. They did not know
*   That even now they might have touched His hand.*

And so at times upon the road of life,
*   I, too, am blind and often fail to see*
That He is ever present at my side,
*   To guide my erring step and comfort me.*

BESIDE THIS SHINING POOL

When, in the cool of evening,
The rose is touched with dew,
And the river mist is rising,
I always think of you.

Here in this cherished garden,
Where dusk-sweet breezes blow,
I see the flowers and winding path,
That we two used to know.

And here beside this shining pool,
Where the lily whitely gleams,
We often came to sit and talk
And dream our foolish dreams.

And oh, I wish I could have the peace
That I knew before you came,
For a garden with you no longer here
Can never be the same.

QUICKLY YOU CAME

Quickly you came and sat by my side,
And put your head in your hands and cried.
Seeing you weeping there,
I bent and kissed your hair.
"Loving you so I can never forget,"
You said to me that night...and yet,
Looking toward a distant day,
I knew it would be this way.

The south wind blew the fragrant rain
Softly against the window pane,
And while you said, "I can never forget,"
I saw the screen all shining and wet.
I knew you'd forget, but after the years,
I would remember your words, your tears;
I would remember with grief and pain,
Your words and your tears and the smell of the rain.

OF THIS I AM SURE

I shall never see you again--of this I am sure.
Once I thought I could not endure
This place without you. Now I find
I do not mind--
For there is enough of beauty left and tasks to do...
(I swear I am done with even the thought of you.)

I shall set these eager, empty hands to wind the clock,
To polish my candlesticks, to sew me a dimity frock.
I shall watch the cardinal build in the apple tree;
Call on my neighbor and borrow a recipe;
Take long walks in the silent, green-arched wood.
And fling myself on the fragrant earth and call it good.

When silence grows too thick at night,
I shall go out from my roof; of thin moonlight
Fashion a silver cloak and for an hour wear
A green star in my hair;
Then dance until I am tired and sure of sleep,
But before I go in, I shall sit by the lilacs and weep.

"GO TO THE ANT..."

I saw a polished, blue-black ant today,
Making a zig-zag, yet unfaltering way
Through a matted jungle of wiry grass.
Transfixed, I stooped to watch it pass,
While holding well above its shining head
A more than life-size store of daily bread.

Rising, I pondered again the burdens of all
God's earth-bound creatures, great and small;
For I widowed young, and in Depression years,
After drying frequent and unbidden tears,
Slowly, painfully had to learn
In those lean times how difficult to earn
(Trying the while to keep aloft my head)
For self and two small children shoes and bread.

VILLANELLE

Ah, life was sweet in old Pompeii,
Glad song and laughter swelled the air,
When death rained fire that summer day.

Strong slaves pulled carts of sun-dried hay
And felt the kitchen wench's stare.
Ah, life was sweet in old Pompeii.

The potter wrought fine urns of clay;
The freedman loitered on the square,
When death rained fire that summer day.

Bright flowers caught the sun's first ray;
The lady found her courtyard fair.
Ah, life was sweet in old Pompeii.

The children scurried out to play,
Secure within the watchdog's care,
When death rained fire that summer day.

Long centuries untouched they lay,
Now street and "talking wall" are bare.
Ah, life was sweet in old Pompeii,
When death rained fire that summer day.

SPRING INCIDENT: APPALACHIA

Climbing the trail to the jagged crest of the ridge,
Coming once more to the sylvan shelter where
The fragile trailing arbutus rosily blushed
And subtly perfumed the crystalline spring air,
I was happy a moment, and, bending down,
Touching the petals, I felt a quickened glow
That here so pink and delicate a flower
Should bravely bloom above the lingering snow.

Descending then with lightened heart and step
Into the narrow somber glen
Where the foot bridge crossed the hurtling stream,
I met the four gaunt mountain men;
Their faces grimed and blackened, but for rings
About the eyes now grown intensely bright.
Between them, solemnly, they bore a form
Carefully wound in a sheet starkly white.

Under the hill, where the dainty arbutus flower
Sweetly perfumed the eager spring's clean breath,
A man had gone early that morning laughing
And brave into his sunless chamber of death.

FROM A WINDOW: ST. MARY'S

Up and down, in the corridor at my back
The nurses go; snowy primness of dress
Cannot conceal exuberance of youth.
In shadow-softness, nuns float by,
Their faces fixed in benign concern.
In her narrow bed, my mother moves
Pale, moth-wing hands above her breast.
Below, in the rose-bordered garden,
A mockingbird teeters audaciously
Atop the head of the lofty marble Christ,
And, in giddy abandon, flings hosannas heavenward.

Oh, Christ of the lonely corridor,
Of the ordered garden court,
Can it be that my eyes but invent
A smile of tender merriment
About those lips of stone?

AT THE GRAVES OF MY PARENTS

Beneath the pine the blue-starred myrtle blooms;
Stone angels tip their wings in suppliant prayer.
Near me, your gentle spirits seem to brood
And whisper in the ambient April air.
Mother, Father, still the sparrow's song
Across the greening field comes clear and sweet,
While restless, glinting waters of Norris Lake
Lap in even rhythm at your feet.

Sheltered by the Cumberlands, the village school,
The country Gothic church, the dear home place:
Oh, Mother, I see you stitch the bright patch quilts,
Or sew my Sunday dress with tucks and lace.
And when we walked the silent winter woods
Together, Father, you always knew,
Deftly brushing clean, deep snow aside,
Where scarlet wintergreen berries grew.

The tapestry that weaves your simple ways,
In memory still brightens all my days.

RECOVERING FROM ILLNESS IN SPRING

Coming out of the fever, the ache in my bones,
I grope for my scuffs, and set my feet on the floor,
Fumble into my robe and, haltingly,
Step outside the sun-warmed open door.

The dog leaps up. His eager eyes speak love
And glad relief as he bounds to take his stand
Beside me and squiggle his cool, wet nose
Into my welcoming, outstretched hand.

Swift changes in a week have come about:
Solid ice that sealed the bird bath gone,
The weeping willow showing tender green,
And Johnny-jump-ups carpeting the lawn.

Returning starlings that observed me once
With hostile yellow eye and cunning leer,
Wobbling clumsily across the grass,
Now suddenly are comical and dear.

HAIKU

Five yellow tulips,
Gold cups mixing sun and rain,
Nectar for the gods.

CACHEPOT

Why, on this particular night,
In the lamp's first glow of light,
Do I see anew this small flower pot
That for years has followed our household about?
A wedding gift of the Great Depression times
(We had to count our nickels and dimes),
Chosen with care, I am sure,
At our only department store.
The genteel owners called customers by name,
Their courteous service always the same;
But through changing times and changing hands, to date
"Swallowed up" by some giant conglomerate.
Here no priceless Dresden urn,
But prettily wreathed around
By leaves and tendrils of a green vine,
Splashed with red blossoms of simple design.
From season to season through sad, through sunny hours,
Holding countless bouquets of garden flowers.
At times a receptacle for scissors, pencils, pens,
Paper clips and unidentified keys,
But on this night it holds--mostly memories.

FOR REMEMBRANCE

The mellow autumn days are here again;
    Blue leaf smoke like an incense, fills the air
To mingle with the smell of ripened fruit,
    And brooding silence lingers everywhere.

From slim white arms the graceful sycamore
    Drops shining leaves into an amber stream;
At night, a hunter's moon is in the sky,
    And on the meadowland the witch fires gleam.

A sense of peace pervades the drowsy earth
    As maples don their gold and scarlet dress;
And when the brief grey days of winter come at last
    I shall remember all of autumn's loveliness.

Alma at UN – 1958

Robert at work – 1950

Liz and Cindy – 1948

Alma, Betty and Bobby
(Liz and Robert) – 1935

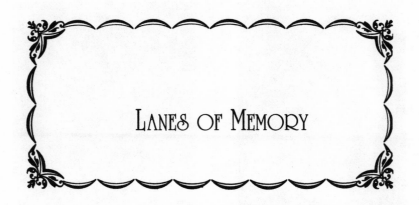

LANES OF MEMORY

Hayes Brown and friend – 1976

First Snow
Katy – 1966

The Cooking Lesson
Hayes and Ross – 1980

Ross and Katy Mynatt – 1968

Christmas with Grandchildren

QUESTIONS

Oh, little Christmas Tree,
   How do you like to wear
A shining tinsel dress,
   And a silver star in your hair?

Do you not like to hold,
   In your arms, the jolly toys
That make this such a merry time
   For happy girls and boys?

Oh, little Christmas Tree,
   I should really like to know--
Do you miss your forest friends,
   And the starlit hill, and the snow?

Or would you rather stand
   In the glow of our warm firelight,
And share in the mirth and joy
   That are ours this Christmas night?

WHAT WILL CHRISTMAS MEAN?

What will Christmas mean to you,
    And what will Christmas mean to me?
Gifts done up in silver and blue,
    A green and fragrant star-crowned tree.

Open wood fire, bright leaping flames,
    Red poinsettias, soft candlelight,
Friendly voices calling our names,
    And children singing "Silent Night."

An ancient story retold again
    Of the Christ-child born in a manger bed,
Of angels and shepherds and Three Wise Men,
    And Mary caressing a baby's head.

Holly wreaths and glistening snow,
    Ah, these will be Christmas for you and me.
Good will and laughter and song we'll know,
    But what of the children across the sea?

GIFT OF THE SHEPHERD BOY

I had no gift for the dear Christ Child,
No gold, no spices sweet,
No cuddly toy for His arms to hold,
No shoes to warm His feet.
And so from the vineyard on the hill,
I have fashioned a wreath of vines,
Adorned it with scarlet berries,
And cones from tall green pines.

Now I follow His star and come this night
To hang my simple gift at His head,
Then kneel in wondering adoration
As he sleeps in a soft straw-bed.

FOR CHRISTMAS EVE

Tonight the quiet, star-lit country lanes
>*And city streets are filled with soft, clean snow,*
And all the footsteps that resounded yesterday
>*Are muted now as people come and go.*

Within, the tree is draped in tinsel dress,
>*The fire of fragrant logs is warm and bright.*
Tall candles glow upon the window sills,
>*And all seems merry in this house tonight.*

But that our happiness may be complete,
>*And that our home this Christmas Eve be truly*
>*blest,*
O little Child of ancient Bethlehem,
>*Come in tonight, we pray, and be our Guest!*

CITY SIDEWALK

The music of bells is faintly heard
Above the drifting snow;
The shoppers walk by with muted step,
And traffic is hushed and slow.

The stylish lady descends with care
From her waiting limousine,
Then draws her furs about her throat,
For the winter air grows keen.

With eagerness, she makes her way
To the elegant polished door
That admits her into welcoming warmth
Of the city's finest store.

While standing outside, alone and small,
By the window, Oh, see these two!
Ignored by all who pass them by
On the bustling avenue;

Thinly clad in shapeless coats
Of the numberless, innocent poor,
Enchanted by toys they can never own,
In the city's finest store.

THE PURCHASE

Snow was falling softly that afternoon
When I heard a timid knock at my kitchen door.
There he stood, little shivering country boy,
Dressed in hand-me-downs of the poor.

"Good evenin', ma'am! I caught this rabbit,
And wondered if you would buy it.
You see it is young and good to eat.
Do you think you would like to try it?"

I gave him some change; whistling he went,
And pleased that I had not refused him.
Oh, beautiful to see, leaping across the snow,
Was the rabbit then, when I loosed him.

FIRST SNOW

A little early it came this year,
Or so it seemed to me,
The first snow, beginning at noon
Quite unexpectedly.

Now up and down this friendly street,
Laughing, from every door,
Wearing caps and sweaters bright,
The happy children pour.

How swiftly gate and roof and tree
Are changed before our eyes,
While still the magic whiteness swirls
From leaden, wintry skies.

Though I live to a hundred, I shall see
Nothing more beautiful
Than first snow, soft as down of a swan,
Whiter than baby lamb's wool.

WINDY NIGHT

At night, when I
　　Am safe in bed,
With the light turned out
　　And my prayer said,
I like to lie
　　Quite still, and hear
The wind go blowing
　　Far and near.

Up in the pines
　　It softly moans,
Then down in the hollow
　　It loudly groans.
High on the hill,
　　Like a lion, it roars,
Now it is knocking
　　At all our doors.
Now it is tapping
　　My window pane,
Then around the corner,
　　It is gone again.

Oh, the wind is bold,
　　And the wind is strong.
I like to hear
　　Its lusty song,
When I am safe
　　In my cozy bed,
With the wooly blanket
　　Pulled up to my head.

WILD DUCKS

When fog hangs low upon the marsh,
　　The wild ducks settle and stay
Until the sun breaks through the mist,
And again they can find their way.

I hold my breath and creep to the marsh
　　To see them gliding there,
And the beauty of wild things fills my heart
　　As it fills the listening air.

At the sound of a snapping twig,
　　Startled, they rise and fly,
Their bodies, black notes of wild music
　　Against a grey winter sky.

And now, on your way to blue lagoons,
　　My wish to you for luck
In escaping the hunter's arm,
　　Brave little green-feathered duck.

WINTER PLANS

Said the robin to the sparrow:
    "Don't you know it's quite the thing,
For folk who want to be in style,
    To go South until spring?"

The sparrow shook his saucy head
    And smiled a sparrow smile,
"I'll take a good snow storm," said he,
"I do not care for style."

The robin drew her eyebrows up
    And murmured, "You poor thing!
Give me the sunshine of the South--
See you again next spring."

"BIG APPLE": 1958

We took a trip to New York town,
    And such fine sights to see!
Great ships coming in to the harbor
    Past the Statue of Liberty.

We toured the UN Building,
    Tall shrine to a peaceful world;
While above us the colorful flags
    Of the United Nations unfurled.

In the Plaza we saw the skaters
    Glide merrily hand in hand.
In their bright-hued dress on the glistening ice,
    They were figures in fairyland.

We ate cheesecake at Lindy's,
    And shopped in famous stores;
We saw the fierce stone lions crouched
    By the Public Library doors.

And, oh, the mounted policeman who braved
    The flowing traffic's command,
Then reined in, permitting his horse to eat
    A lump of sugar from my hand!

WALK SOFTLY

My pretty, light-hearted lass,
    Pause wherever you are;
Consider this ancient advice:
    "Walk softly and go far."

Let your touch be gentle,
    For gently, my lass,
Apple blossom petals touch
    The spring's new grass.

And let your words, my dear,
    Be soft and slow,
Remembering the soundlessness
    Of drifting snow.

Then walk in velvet shoes, my lass,
    Of such are silent things:
Purple dusk and moths that go
    On chartreuse wings.

COLLEGE GIRL

She hurries along, books on her arm,
Dressed in sweater and skirt all neat.
Leaves of autumn, scarlet and gold,
Tumble about her feet.

A dream in her heart, mirth in her eyes,
Sunlight warm on her shining hair;
Growing in wisdom day by day,
Learning to think, to do, to share.

On the step beneath the Gothic arch
Where the ivy clings, I see her stand,
And I think of the hundreds like her who grace
Hall and campus throughout our land.

SOME THINGS I LIKE

I like old cupboards that smell of spice,
  I like new pennies and sound advice.
I like white ducks, old glass and clocks,
  I like blue ribbons and organdy frocks.

I like airplanes. I like perfume,
  Irish crochet and red clover bloom,
Boxwoods and rabbits, a clear mountain stream,
  Strawberry shortcake with heaps of whipped cream.

I like pine cones, I like autumn rain,
  Firelight and candles and wide fields of grain.
I like a brown path that climbs a tall hill,
  And on a summer night, a plaintive whippoorwill.

ROBERT AT SIX AND THE BEAN VINE

Robert planted a small brown bean
    In a red small pot,
And set it on the window ledge
    In a sun-warmed spot.

Each day he gave it water,
    And soon a tender sprout,
Above the moist, dark earth,
    Shook two pale leaves out.

Up around the window frame,
    Robert trained his vine;
Oh, such a leafy drapery
    Was, truly, very fine!

And Robert's friends from blocks away
    Came to see how tall
A green vine, a bean vine
    Could climb a window wall.

Liz, TWA "Air Hostess" – 1955

Robert, U.S. Air Force – 1955

AIRPLANE

A far-away drone is heard.
       Then suddenly out of the blue,
Two gleaming silver wings
       Come hurtling into view.

Timid fowls in the sun
       Flee to a sheltering cover,
Hushed and frightened they stand
       As the monster bird flies over.

Boys and girls at play look up,
       And with dreaming eyes they gaze
As it rapidly disappears
       Into the distant haze.

Soon at their play again
       But still the dream remains--
Some day they too shall fly
       Through space in shining planes.

A BOY IN SPRING

In spring a boy likes to fling his books aside
And leap and run and hide
As wild things of the forest do,
And walk barefoot across a meadow wet with dew.
A boy likes to sit beside a drowsy stream;
He may not catch a single fish, but he can dream.
He likes to throw himself upon the grass
And watch the brown ants pass,
And, without thinking, chew
A tender blade or two.
Then looking upward follow with keen sight
The wild geese flying north in eager flight.

In spring a boy likes the wind and sun,
For there are many things to see and do,
And golden hours seem but precious few
From early morning till the day is done.

CAFETERIA

I placed a sheltered feeding board
*   Upon my window sill,*
An invitation to the birds
*   To come and feast at will.*

And now from early dawn till dusk,
*   They fly a wintry mile,*
Through rain or snow to serve themselves,
*   In cafeteria style.*

I HEARD GOD

When I was out in the yard today
I heard God, I heard Him say,
"Hi, Betty!" Like Uncle Sid, our gardener, you know.
He plants seeds and cuts weeds with a hoe.
I think God and Uncle Sid are swell.
I guess they get along pretty well,
'Cause Uncle Sid tends the flowers,
And God sends the showers.
Well, when I heard Him say
"How're you, Betty?" I answered, "I'm OK."

SHEILAH'S GOOSE

Look, Sheilah! There in the spring-wet grass.
Now who could have turned her loose?
At home with the hens, accepting their scratch,
A horn-blasting, dear white goose.

Came the first winter night, the paddy-paws,
The ruby eyes' fire-glow,
The close frosted breath, one garbled shriek,
Then, stillness of feathers on snow.

"You could have barred the hen house door,"
Pouring hot coffee, tears on her face;
"You could have reminded me," he snapped,
Turning his hands at the stove and taking his place.

Out to the kitchen came Sheilah,
In her night dress and rosy from sleep,
And sensed the hurt in their eyes,
But she did not weep.

Only stood at the pane, her eyes grown great,
But said not a word.
Her silence matched the silence without,
Where lately preened her noisy, proud bird.

THINGS TO BE FORGOTTEN

Oh, do not nourish envy,
    It yields a bitter fruit
That grows to huge proportions
    Once it has taken root.

Forget that disappointment
    And grief have come to you,
But rather store the heart with these:
    The just, the kind, the true.

Forget the loved one's angry word,
    The critic's barbed remark;
Remember pansies in the sun,
    A thrush's song at dark.

SONG FOR EVENING

The stars are nodding flowers that bloom
    In the wide field of the sky;
The moon is a golden wheel that goes
    Rolling noiselessly by.

The wind is asleep in the hollow,
    The cattle are taking their rest,
A tired child climbs the stairway,
    The bird cuddles down in its nest.

The baby lamb at its mother's side,
    Sleeps on the stony hill;
Save for katydids in the trees,
    The night is hushed and still.

The stars are bright flower faces
    That blossom overhead;
Sleep, little bird, in your twiggy nest,
    And sleep, little child, in your bed.

SAVE THE PLANET

This blue dot
Is all we've got!

1990   Alma C. Brown

ABOUT THE AUTHOR

Alma Cleo Childress was born in 1907 and grew up in *Storybook* Powell Valley near LaFollette, Tennessee. She married Alva Ross Brown, President of Johnson Bible College, and after his death in 1941, Mrs. Brown moved to Knoxville, where she resides today.

She is a Phi Kappa Phi and Pi Lambda Theta Honors Graduate of the University of Tennessee. Her teaching career was in the English Departments of University of Tennessee and Milligan College, and at retirement, she was a high school librarian in the Knoxville City School system.

Alma Childress Brown's writing began in the eighth grade. The author has published poetry, feature articles, and stories in various publications and has written an earlier book, *Summer Treasure And Other Poems*. She is active in the National League of American Pen Women - Knoxville Branch, Daughters of the American Revolution -James White Chapter, and other civic organizations. She is a member of First Christian Church. Travel and collecting antiques are special interests.

In addition to a son and daughter of Atlanta and Dallas, respectively, she has three grandchildren.